AF481144

MAKE YOUR SUCCESS

THE 21 RULES FOR YOUNG PROFESSIONALS

DANIEL HEIMLICH

Published by IngramSpark

ISBN: 979-8-218-08722-7

Cover and book design by Banished Rascals Design
www.banishedrascals.com

PRINTED IN THE UNITED STATES OF AMERICA

*Dedicated to
Julia, Sara and Josh*

Contents

"Without continual growth and progress, such words as improvement, achievement and success have no meaning."

— Benjamin Franklin

Introduction

It still amazes me that self-management and professional communication skills are not formally taught in school. Neither are the psychology and attitudes you'll need to thrive in a professional environment. Most schooling is focused on building your knowledge, but not on how to get things done and succeed in the "real world."

Some of these skills you'll acquire through osmosis, maybe by participating in school clubs or other extracurricular programs. If you're lucky, you have a successful parent or other mentor to model yourself after. When you're in the working world, you'll naturally learn more through trial and error, as well as by studying seasoned colleagues and bosses.

But probably no one will ever sit you down and say, "Here are the key principles you'll need to master for a successful professional career."

That's precisely what this book is intended to help you with.

It's hard for me to pinpoint exactly where I learned these techniques. But somehow, through decades of experiences and observation, I formulated and honed a set of principles that are immensely effective. They have propelled my career — and the careers of people I've mentored.

I started jotting down these "rules for success" in a notebook some years ago. Initially, my goal was to define them in a book for my own children as they set out into the professional world.

But as I began to write, I realized that these rules could be helpful for anyone who is early in their career journey. And frankly, I've worked with plenty of people who are well into their 30s, 40s and 50s who would greatly benefit from the principles in this book.

It's a short book. The lessons are quick to understand, but may take a lot of practice to master. You may find it helpful to first read through the book in its entirety, and a few times throughout each year. In the days and weeks in between, you can use the book as a quick-reference tool; just flip to whichever rule addresses the issue you're facing at the time.

If you apply these time-tested principles on a consistent basis, I have no doubt that they will propel your own success.

RULE

1

Build Your
Personal Brand

Your personal brand represents the characteristics that people remember you for. Also known as your professional reputation, it's something you want to manage with intention.

If you're not sure what your personal brand is or could be, here is the key question to ask yourself:

How would you like your managers and colleagues to describe you in private?

Think about it carefully. Be sure it's authentic to you, and that it accurately reflects both your professional aspirations and what you can realistically be known for.

To keep this exercise simple, I suggest capturing your brand in just three words or phrases. My personal brand, which you'll read about more than once in this book, is defined as:

1. Great marketer

2. Creative problem solver

3. Always reliable

Once you've captured your brand, you need to embody and reinforce it. Your communications and decisions should reflect your brand. Your resume should promote your brand. The books and blogs you read, the podcasts you listen to, the classes you take, and the mentors you seek out should sharpen and bolster your brand.

Most importantly, your everyday actions impact your brand. Showing up late to meetings, blowing off commitments, and half-assing projects degrade your personal brand. On the flip side: Over-delivering, always showing up on time, and following through on promises boost your personal brand.

What's your personal brand? Write it down and look at it every day until you have it memorized.

Remember that your brand is written on paper, digital or otherwise. It's not written in cement, and it may evolve over time as your interests and responsibilities change.

One way or the other, you will have a personal brand. Own it.

RULE

2

Give People What They *Need*

Imagine you're at a doctor's appointment. Your doctor enters the exam room and before they say anything, you declare, "Doctor, I have a sinus infection and will need a prescription for antibiotics."

No doctor worth their salt would write a prescription and walk out the door. Instead, they would respond, "Well, tell me more about your symptoms." The doctor would listen, examine you, and then diagnose your condition. They may find you are suffering from allergies and just need some over-the-counter allergy medicine.

Similar scenarios play out in the business world all the time. I can't tell you how many times my boss or a client has said, "This is the problem, and I need you to do X to fix it." They self-diagnose without necessarily knowing the best solution.

One secret power that you have is *you're not them*. You see their challenges through a different lens. They're often too close to the issue, or perhaps they haven't given it enough thought. As a result, your objectivity enables you to see and solve the problem in a way that they cannot.

Furthermore, just doing what you're told affects your brand. You will provide minimal (or maybe no) value, and you might not solve their problem. Almost anyone can do what they're told to do. You're not just arms and legs. Use your brain. Be a constant problem solver. Come back with an alternative solution, a better way of doing things.

You're not just arms and legs. Use your brain. Be a constant problem solver. Come back with an alternative solution, a better way of doing things.

When I work with clients, I advocate strongly for my diagnosis and solution. Even though I'm being paid, I cannot accept moving in a direction that I know is the wrong path. If my recommendation is met with resistance, I'll often come back to my position with evidence in tow.

Of course, if your view fails to make headway, you'll need to support the favored decision — even if you disagree with it. Though your idea wasn't chosen, you should feel good about having contributed to the problem-solving process. By challenging the status quo, you helped the others validate and possibly refine the final chosen direction. Plus, if you made your case with a genuine desire to help the organization (rather than your ego), you'll be respected for it.

A few years ago, I was working with a marketing agency on a big project for one of their clients. The agency and I listened to the client, and towards the end of the meeting the client told us what direction they wanted to go in. It was clear the client didn't know what they needed. But instead of asking for our expert opinion, they just told us what to do.

Later that afternoon, I called the agency. "What the client is asking for isn't going to work," I said.

"Oh, we know," they responded. They didn't care about delivering value; they only cared about collecting a check. It still bothers me to this day.

Throughout my career, I have found that if you just do what people want, you're a commodity. If you give them what they **need** and you take it to the next level, you're adding considerable value.

I've sat in the executive seat as well. As a boss, I've asked people on my team to work on a problem and sometimes "direct" them on how to solve it. However, I don't expect them to just blindly work on it. Stop and think. Does the direction address the issue? Are you working on the real problem? Is there a better way?

Far too many times people have delivered projects to me that don't address the real issue or problem. "Well, that's what you asked for!" they'll respond.

"Don't give me what I ask for — give me what I need," I tell them.

By the way, giving people what they need is one of the fastest ways to build your personal brand.

RULE

3

Expectations
& Communications

Virtually every human interaction you have in a professional setting relates to some expectation.

An expectation can be as small as "I'll be right back," or as big as "I'm going to take us to Mars." Deliver according to the expectation, and you will be trusted. And if you are trusted, you will be sought out for more and bigger opportunities.

Expectations come in different forms. In the workplace they are often related to a promised deliverable within a particular timeframe (delivering a report, launching a product, joining a meeting, etc. by X date). Your personal brand depends on meeting those expectations. Once you are trusted, no one will check on you. Everyone will know that your commitment is good as gold.

After expectations are set, shift into communications mode. Frequently communicate project status and reassure your boss, teammates or client that you will meet the deadline.

If circumstances change and you can't meet expectations, communicate that immediately. The last thing you want is to surprise people (especially your boss).

Likewise, if you are the leader, be sure expectations are clear for your team: Communicate them verbally and in writing. Even when people do not formally report to you, expectation setting is a very powerful management tool. During group meetings, assign tasks to individuals and ask them to acknowledge their commitments. Publicly stating the expectation for each team member holds them accountable to the group.

Always remember: Expectations and communications go hand in hand.

RULE

4

Be Proactive

Just as you should always give people what they need, you should continually look for opportunities to help improve your organization. Don't stop at what you're asked to do or what your job calls for. Go the extra mile in everything you do.

Early in my career, I always had two jobs: the job I was hired to do, and the job I wanted to do. This mindset ensured I wasn't just a cog in the machine, a commodity employee who could be easily replaced.

Instead, I always look to bring additional value to my job and my organization. As you may recall, part of my personal brand is solving problems. Whenever I see a problem (even if it's not my area of responsibility), I fix it. When I see a problem and can't fix it myself, I bring it to someone's attention.

Another aspect of being proactive is making things happen.

When I lived in South Florida many years ago, I was looking for a new job. I found this little software company called Citrix and was really impressed with what they were doing. They were not hiring, but that didn't stop me. I found the contact information for the CEO at the time, Roger Roberts, and emailed him. I didn't hear back, so I called. I still didn't hear back, so I called him every other day. I even dropped off letters at the company's front desk.

One day I called him yet again, and this time Roger answered. As I began introducing myself, he interrupted me. "I know who you are. Anyone who has tried this hard to join the company deserves a chance. I'm going to put you in touch with our head of marketing for an interview."

I succeeded in the interview and became the 88th employee at Citrix. At the time, it was just a $14 million company. When I left six years later, we had more than 2,000 employees and nearly $600 million in revenue.

More than two decades after leaving Citrix, I attended a company reunion. I saw Roger talking to someone and approached them. He interrupted the conversation to give me a big hug. "See this guy?" he asked his friend. "He wouldn't leave me alone until I answered his call!" He still remembered my persistence from so many years ago.

The opportunity to work at Citrix changed the trajectory of my career and my life. And it only came about because I was proactive (and very persistent).

Create the career you want with a proactive attitude. Bonus: It will build your confidence.

RULE

5

Persistence Pays

I attribute the majority of my professional success to persistence. The Citrix story I shared in the previous chapter is just one of many examples of how persistence paid. Persistence alone places you in the top 25% of high achievers.

Unlike many people who follow a traditional job search, I've never been hired via a recruiter or by answering an ad.

I got my first job out of college by literally knocking on doors. I got my next two jobs by calling the companies directly. You already know that persistence got me a job at Citrix. I built my consulting business through persistence as well.

I know how difficult it is to be told no, so switch your definition. When someone tells me no, I hear, "Not right now." I can't tell you the number of times I've turned a "no" into a "yes."

If you want a certain job or to work on a specific project, don't give up. Use your persuasive powers. Show them the facts, reframe what you're asking for, understand the objection, and look for a win-win.

Or maybe you're dealing with a naysayer and need to find a different entry point. Don't let the naysayers get in your way. Find a way around or through them. When I can't get something done because someone is blocking me, I'll immediately log into LinkedIn, find out who the president or CEO of the company is, and reach out to them.

Some years ago, my mother-in-law's doctor prescribed her a medication that her insurance wouldn't cover. She couldn't afford to pay out of pocket, and there were no other alternatives in her health plan. I found the president of the pharmaceutical company on LinkedIn, and I contacted him. "Oh, we have a program for seniors who can't afford the medication," he said. Of course, they didn't advertise this program. But in the end, she got free medication from the company for years.

I wasn't gifted academically. But I was always a great problem solver, always proactive and always persistent. Those are the things that have propelled me through life.

The author Wayne Dyer talks about ducks and eagles. Ducks just do their jobs. Eagles soar and take it to the next level.

Be an eagle.

RULE

6

Attack from the Top

People in positions of authority have the credibility and power to get things done. The story of my mother-in-law's free medication demonstrates this perfectly. Sometimes you need to attack from the top.

You don't want to come out waving a bat every single time you can't get what you need. Choose your moments. It needs to be important (life-saving medication versus a dinner reservation at a Michelin-starred restaurant) and done in a way that's sensitive to the people you are leapfrogging over.

I strongly suggest limiting this tactic when it comes to dealing with people in your own organization. However, sometimes it's necessary. If you can't get critical data from a colleague you're working closely with, be transparent. Say, "I understand you might not have the authority to make this decision, so I'm going to reach out to your manager." Notably, this one statement might be all the motivation your colleague needs. "Miraculously," they'll find a way to deliver on their own, so you won't have to attack from the top.

That colleague may be a blocker. They may have their own agenda and fiercely protect it. Or they might not have the confidence to move the ball forward, and are just doing what's expected of them. As I mentioned at the end of the previous chapter, those people are ducks.

When you're faced with a blocker, find the eagles in that organization. They're the ones with the influence to help you.

During my time at the company Blackboard, I had an inside view of what happened when customers contacted our CEO directly. They were disgruntled about something, and the CEO would demand an answer by the end of the day. Suddenly an army of people were working on the problem. A person of authority can mobilize the right people and cut through the red tape, so you can get your answer faster.

RULE

7

Prepare for Every Meeting

Meetings are opportunities to move the ball forward on a project or decision. Never step into a meeting without being prepared. Generally, it takes just a few minutes to organize your thoughts and be ready. As I like to say, a few minutes of planning is worth hours of aggravation.

First, have a clear goal in mind: What are you trying to achieve? Write it down. Second, review background information to refresh your memory. Third, write down each of the items you'd like to cover, along with any key points you want to make.

Just a few key words are enough to jog your memory. (In other words, don't write long sentences.) Amazingly, you may never need to check your notes, because the process itself mentally prepares you.

While I was writing this book, I didn't follow my own advice, and it was embarrassing. A few weeks before, I had submitted a proposal to a lucrative potential client, which I now needed to present. Before the big client meeting, the company's CFO wanted to make sure we were aligned and requested a call to sync up.

Never step into a meeting without being prepared. Generally, it takes just a few minutes to organize your thoughts and be ready.

I wasn't prepared at all. As we chatted, I was frantically searching through emails and files to find the proposal. The CFO would ask me specific questions, and I'd answer, but I was fumbling. I asked to go through the entire proposal again, which was a big waste of his time. It was obvious I wasn't prepared, and it impacted my personal brand.

A few minutes of preparation can greatly boost your efficiency and make meetings much more effective for everyone.

<u>RULE</u>

8

Always Take Notes

Now that you're prepared for that meeting, don't stop there. Take notes. There's no need to try to remember everything.

Think of your notebook (or notes application) as an outside filing system for your brain. With so many things happening in your life, these notes will jog your memory. But frankly, you may never have to look at them. The action of taking notes will boost your recall.

I use Evernote, and the application literally holds thousands of my notes. Physically writing something is better for your memory, but I type faster than I write. Plus, digital apps have built-in search and filing capabilities, making it much easier to find the information you need quickly.

When I'm taking notes, sometimes I find that I'm essentially taking dictation and writing everything the other person is saying, word for word. I'll review the notes and find gems of information that I somehow didn't hear when I was furiously typing.

Taking notes is also a sign of respect for the people who are talking. It makes them feel good: "I have something important enough to say that it is being written down!"

The reverse is true as well. I recall interviewing someone for a job, and as I told them about job duties, company culture, my expectations, etc., they just sat there. "I wonder if they're capturing what I'm saying — or even paying attention? Maybe they aren't interested in working here," I thought.

Never enter a meeting without a notepad (paper or electronic). If you use a laptop, move it off to the side, so there is not a "wall" between you and the person you're speaking with. And please don't ever use a phone to take notes in a meeting. Maybe Gen Z and Millennials won't mind, but most others will see it as junior league.

Whether you take notes to help with recall, uncover new information, or show respect, this simple task will help build your personal brand.

RULE

9

Set High Standards

My grandfather Papa Charlie used to say, "There is no sense in doing a job unless you do it right."

Papa Charlie was an insurance salesman. I don't think he even finished high school, but he was very successful. I spent a lot of time with him as a kid and watched him fix things up around the house. He was very methodical in his work. He taught me to set high standards, take pride in my efforts, and never do anything half-assed.

You're not going to enjoy everything you need to do at work. But if you're going to exert the energy, be sure you're putting your time to good use. Others will take note that you are an achiever who cares about doing a good job. They'll know they can count on you.

Steve Jobs noted a life-long lesson from his father, who was a skilled craftsman. When his father built something, the work was pristine whether you could see it or not (like the bottom of a table). Steve recalled in an interview, "When you're a carpenter making a beautiful chest of drawers, you're not going to use a piece of plywood on the back, even though it faces the wall and nobody will ever see it. For you to sleep well at night, the aesthetic, the quality, has to be carried all the way through."

Ultimately Steve Jobs incorporated this ethic into the product design culture at Apple, making it one of the most loved and highly valued companies in the world.

Another famous saying I like is, "Measure twice, cut once." Check and double-check your work. Be precise. Often that means putting the work aside for a few hours or overnight. Come back to it later, and you'll be amazed at what a fresh mind will reveal.

Take personal pride in everything you do. Set high standards for yourself and those around you.

10

Go Slow to Go Fast

When you learn a new skill, you always start with the fundamentals. When you learn to toss a basketball, you learn it's all in the wrist. When you learn how to golf, you learn it's not about the speed of the stroke but how your club connects with the ball.

LeBron James and Tiger Woods make their respective sports, basketball and golf, look easy. LeBron is quick on the court and tosses the ball with finesse. Tiger swings his club so fast that you can't see it — and you definitely cannot see the ball flying toward the green. They went slow at first, so they could go fast now.

If you go fast before you're ready, you will make mistakes and/or cut corners. You will make a mess, and you might have to start all over again. As a result, things will take longer than they should.

Some years ago, my company had a last-minute opportunity to exhibit at an important trade show. I assigned one of my staff people — who we'll call Sue — to handle the project on a tight but achievable deadline. "I'm on it!" she said.

A week later, as I was walking by her desk, Sue excitedly waved me over. On the computer was a rendering of the finished booth design, which the vendor had already started manufacturing. As Sue sat smiling, I reviewed the booth design and noticed that a wall was placed on the wrong side — which would obstruct the view from the main traffic aisle. Even worse, there was a typo in the signage.

Sue was apologetic, "I'm so sorry... I was rushing everything to meet the deadline." When we called the vendor, the rep said it was too late to make the changes in time for delivery. Fortunately, when I contacted their president (See Rule 6: "Attack from the Top"), they remedied the situation. But it cost us dearly. We ended up paying thousands more to redo the booth and expedite shipping.

In her earnestness to move fast and make the deadline, Sue missed critical details. The result: Everything took longer and cost more.

We live in a very fast-paced world. But you can be more effective by slowing the game down. Take a deep breath. Step back from the situation. Determine the step-by-step plan. Be present. Then carefully execute your task.

Go slow to go fast.

RULE

11

Write It to Understand It

During my career, I have found that writing down my thoughts and ideas is the best way to process information and even expand on it. I have written notes to my bosses, colleagues and partners, and I have written just for myself. Either way, I have often come through with a new perspective.

Sometimes when I need to clear my head, I'll take a notecard and pen for a walk. Out in the fresh air and away from the daily hubbub, I find that my thinking flows more easily. It's remarkably effective self-therapy.

Writing is also a helpful outlet when you're angry. Write that email, reflect on the message, and let your emotions settle. Don't send it. Instead, decide on next steps or a more level-headed response.

If you don't enjoy writing, ask someone to serve as a sounding board. That person might not bring value or new ideas to the conversation. But as you talk about your idea, you're processing it and gaining clarity.

Sometimes when I need to clear my head, I'll take a notecard and pen for a walk. Out in the fresh air ... I find that my thinking flows more easily.

Get in the habit of writing it — or talking it out. This habit will serve you well.

RULE

12

Write Well

Rough notes for yourself is fine, but you need to be a great writer for others.

I write well thanks to two of my college professors. I remember my very first paper at Tulane University — typed on a typewriter and covered in white-out. I worked so hard on it, and was shocked to learn I got a D. I went to talk to the professor, and she said, "That is not a college-level paper."

And then there was Professor Harl, an internationally recognized authority in Byzantine and Roman history. I loved his classes — they were always packed — yet every paper I turned in to him was returned with comments in red ink all the way through.

Both professors were top-notch editors. They taught me how to effectively organize and communicate my ideas. I've been working on improving my writing ever since.

WRITING WELL COMES DOWN TO SEVEN FUNDAMENTALS.

Keep it short

Good writers make their points using the least number of words. Continually edit yourself and take extraneous words and information out. (Be careful about falling in love with a word or phrase, because you might need to toss it.)

There are exceptions to this rule. You might need to add color to get your point across better, or you might need to provide background information for context. That's OK. You can still be succinct.

Speaking of which, both sentences and paragraphs should be short. The rule of thumb is less than 20 words per sentence and three sentences or fewer per paragraph. Again, there are exceptions, but do your best to stick to these guidelines.

Write like you talk

So many people try to use big words to sound smart, and I always think, "Just get to the point." Your email is not a PhD dissertation. Write like you speak, use common phrases, and use informal sentence structure when it's appropriate.

Grab your readers' attention

What you have to say is important, and you only have seconds to get someone's attention. Don't bury your main point. Provide it up front.

You especially need to make that first (most important) sentence count. So for goodness sake, don't waste it with "Hi, my name is so-and-so..." You want to capture their interest from the start.

Now that they're paying attention, remember that the purpose of every sentence is to get the person to read the next sentence. That's worth repeating: *The purpose of every sentence is to get the person to read the next sentence.* For an email, that means you have to deliver on what you promise in the subject line. It's all about expectations and communications!

Write for your reader

Whenever you write anything, make sure it's from the standpoint of what's important to the reader – NOT you. It's a bit of a chess game. The reader has their own priorities, and you need to navigate through those to get your message – your priority – in front of them.

Take the time to understand your readers' priorities and motivations so you can address them in your writing.

Make one point

No one will remember a list of five points in your message, so choose the one that is most important. Make ONE point in your message. Include ONE concept in each paragraph. Share ONE idea in each sentence.

Write scannable content

For longer messages, add subheads and **bold** text so people can scan and quickly find the core content. Make good use of headlines, which may be the only thing your audience reads. And rather than burying long lists in the body copy, promote key ideas with bullet points that are easier to scan and absorb.

Be persuasive

Almost everything in business (and life) is about selling. If you're not selling a product, you're selling a service, an idea, yourself. You have to get people to buy in, which means you must be persuasive. More on that in the next chapter.

The bottom line: The way you write is a reflection of your personal brand. Learn to do it well. And take the time to do it well.

13

Everyone's a Salesperson

Selling is a core skill that everyone needs. Whether or not you're actually paid to sell, a lot of your job (and success) will be about selling… selling yourself at an interview, pitching a new idea to your boss, persuading a room full of your teammates to see another point of view, or giving a presentation.

I'm going to let you in on a secret about selling: The most important thing about selling is *listening* — not talking. Selling is more about being a detective than it is about pitching.

Listening requires you to ask great questions to analyze and understand the root drivers of your target's needs. (See Rule 18, "Questions Are Your Secret Weapons.") What do they care about? What do they say they want, and what do they need? (See Rule 2, "Give People What They Need.")

It is critical to figure out the "prime motivators" that drive them personally and emotionally. As a salesperson, your job is to tactfully probe until you get to their needs and what will appeal to them emotionally.

Let's say you're a car salesperson. A new customer walks in one morning, and he says, "I'm looking for a car with better gas mileage and acceleration." You ask more questions and learn that he has a new girlfriend and is still driving his grandmother's hand-me-down clunker with ripped velour seats.

When it comes to sales, remember: Listen. Confirm their needs. Align your pitch to their needs. Share evidence that supports your claims.

You continue talking and start piecing together the full story. Once you think you understand his motivators, you repeat back what you've heard: "It sounds like you're looking for a car that handles well and has a more high-end look." (You might avoid adding, "And that will impress your girlfriend.")

You can also ask, "Is there anything else that's important that I missed?" If he has more to add — maybe he prefers a blue car over any other color — repeat back the new information.

Now that you understand his underlying motivations, you can shape your sales pitch to his particular needs. Don't bother talking about features he doesn't care about, like trunk capacity. Focus on the car's comfortable interior, acceleration, and prestige of the brand.

Besides listening and aligning your value proposition according to the target's needs, you need evidence (data, proof points, use cases, etc.) to support your claims and reasoning. Do your homework and be prepared. If possible, use visuals (like charts) to support your claims.

If you're interviewing for a new job, do your homework. Maybe you learn that the job will also have some marketing responsibilities. You can share successful marketing campaigns you've worked on in the past. Let your prospective boss know how you will support their own success.

When it comes to sales, remember: Listen. Confirm their needs. Align your pitch to their needs. Share evidence that supports your claims.

Everyone needs to be a salesperson. Especially you.

Daniel Heimlich

RULE

14

How to Build a Team

If you want to build a great team, don't focus too much on a candidate's resume. Resumes show baseline qualifications, but they don't provide insights about how the person will work on your team. Don't get too enamored by the candidate's degree or job experience. You need to uncover their core skills, attitude, and character.

Every time I interview someone, I ask them if they are an inventor, organizer, socializer, or thinker. Typically, I don't define the terms for them. I'm more interested in hearing the candidate's take.

However, for the purpose of this book, here are my definitions:

Inventor: You can weave concepts together, view things from a new perspective, and solve problems. You are also comfortable living with some chaos.

Organizer: You add structure to the chaos, so you (and those on your team) can understand and act on ideas or information. You like making lists and schedules.

Socializer: You're a collaborator and prefer to be around and work directly with others. You're likely an extrovert who is the last to leave a party.

Thinker: You are highly analytical and like to go deep. Diving into information and looking at data from many points of view is your thing.

Which type are you?

An effective and successful team contains a mix of inventors, organizers, socializers, and thinkers. I'm an inventor, so I always look for organizers to complement me and create structure out of my ideas.

Once you know who you are dealing with, life becomes easier. If your group is balanced, you have a full arsenal of skills. But you need to recognize that each type has their limitations too.

An inventor will constantly throw out ideas. An organizer might start a project before they have all the information. A socializer might struggle to work independently, and a thinker might hyperfocus on inconsequential details.

Know what you are. Know what your team is. Play to everyone's strengths.

RULE

15

Treat Everyone with Dignity

We are all human. We all have things going on at work, in our personal world, and in our inner world. We all have insecurities and egos. Some people have more armor around them than others, but everyone deserves to be treated with dignity no matter the situation.

How often have you read a story about a famous celebrity and thought, "Wow, they have it all together." They don't. Material wealth does not shield them from disappointment, regret, or the consequences of questionable decisions.

People at work may not share everything happening in their worlds, so don't assume they're all sunshine and roses on the inside. Recognize that they are human. Even if you don't like them or have to deliver bad news, treat them delicately.

Years ago, one of my team members was a big burly guy —
I called him the Viking. He was very personable, enthusiastic, and
wanted to do well, but he could never get it together. If he wasn't
making another mistake, he was taking a smoke break. Numerous
conversations to get him on track went nowhere, and eventually
I had to let him go. When I delivered the news — gently and with
compassion — he cried like a baby. It was terrible.

Sometimes a person isn't cut out for that particular job.
Michael Jordan, who is arguably the greatest basketball player ever,
was a mediocre baseball player. He gave it his all to join the big
leagues, but he couldn't cut it. We all have our gifts!

I also encourage you to avoid backing someone into a corner.
Don't try to win at the expense of someone else's dignity. Maybe
you'll bolster your public brand, but maintaining your humanity is
even more critical. When you look in the mirror, you want to see
a person of integrity. Never promote yourself at the expense of
someone's dignity.

It may be hard sometimes, but follow the golden rule: Treat
others as you would have them treat you.

Respond, Don't React

My family would be the first to point out that responding, not reacting, is not a strength of mine. And they'd be right.

If you feel offended, it's so easy to let your emotions run away and bark back. Our natural tendency is to jump in and defend our dignity. When someone questions my integrity — a key part of my personal brand — I am instantly triggered.

Early in my career, I was assigned a new boss. He was clearly in over his head, and he hired an outside consulting firm to help him run things. The day before he was leaving for a two-week vacation, he informed me that the outside firm would be taking over a major project I'd been working on for months.

He was questioning my capabilities, and I lost it. I verbally attacked him in the hallway. A lot of people heard it too. At the time,

I felt my reaction was justified. After all, who was this "idiot" telling me what to do? But looking back, I'm embarrassed.

Just because you are "right" does not mean you should react. Try to never lose your cool. Being in control of your emotions keeps you in command of the situation.

One simple and effective technique I've learned: Take a deep breath, pause, and ask a question. This ensures that you'll respond rather than react.

Be aware of your personal triggers, and keep in mind that an upsetting email or remark might be a misunderstanding. What your boss or colleague is trying to say and how you're interpreting it can be two different things. Before you react, attempt to see things from their point of view and what they're attempting to convey.

Also keep in mind that you can become more prone to react as your career progresses and you gain more confidence in your role. You might think that because you've been successful, you can get away with reacting. Nope.

Respond, don't react.

17

Questions Are Your Secret Weapons

Questions are much more powerful than statements. Questions can soften a statement and create a dialogue, allowing you to make a point without sounding accusatory and enable you to learn new information. They can also shift the tone of a relationship.

Years ago, I had a colleague who would regularly storm into my office with the force of a firehose to share his latest idea. My reaction was often defensive, with a statement like, "Yeah, we tried that last year, and it didn't work." I was being disrespectful, and possibly missing a great idea. So, I put a post-it note on my computer that said, "Pause — Question."

This was my reminder to pause before responding and instead ask a question, such as, "How would this be different from what we tried last time?" or "Can you tell me more about that?" or "Can we set a time to discuss this tomorrow?" It changed our relationship. He felt like I was engaging with him and cared about what he had to say.

There are many situations in which questions become a secret weapon. In a tense situation, you can lower the volume. Tension between people often happens because someone feels misunderstood. So instead of clashing with a statement, try this: "Maybe I'm missing something. Can you help me understand better?"

Questions are the most powerful device in your communications arsenal. They enable you to steer the direction of conversations, achieve mutual understanding, overcome stalemates, and persuade others.

Questions also allow you to buy time, learn more, and gather your thoughts so you can respond carefully. During a meeting with a potential client, they might ask me, "How are you going to help us?" If this is the first time we're talking, I might not know yet. In this case, I can respond with a probing question like, "What prompted you to give me a call?"

Similarly, questions are phenomenal ways of steering conversations. If someone asked me, "How much did you earn last year?" I would be very taken aback. But I'd also guess there is more to that question. I would reply, "Why do you ask?" It could be that their daughter is interested in going out on her own as a marketing consultant, and they are helping her gather income information.

Questions can help you be more persuasive. If I'm selling something and getting a strong objection, I've learned to lob this grenade: "It sounds like you're not interested in resolving this problem right now. Am I reading that right?" Ninety percent of the time, they'll answer, "No, it's not that way at all." You can then ask more questions, gather more information, and persuade them to buy.

Questions are the most powerful device in your communications arsenal. They enable you to steer the direction of conversations, achieve mutual understanding, overcome stalemates, and persuade others.

Do you see what I'm saying? :-)

Daniel Heimlich

RULE

18

Maintain Your Momentum

A friend put me in touch with Deborah, a CEO who needed some help. We had a great conversation. At the conclusion, Deborah said, "I love everything you talked about. I want you to meet our sales director."

After the meeting, I immediately sent Deborah an email that went far beyond a simple thank you. I reiterated the challenges she mentioned, explained why I was able to address them, and let her know that I had already reached out to her sales director.

The meeting with the sales director went well, too. Once again, I followed up with Deborah to let her know what I learned and share a few early ideas I thought could address their challenges.

I was maintaining momentum.

At this point, Deborah requested a proposal. But I insisted on another meeting, which I knew would solidify the relationship. During that meeting, I presented the case for why I was the best person for the project, along with examples. She then started selling *me* on why I should work for *them*.

Once you get forward movement and have someone engaged, you need to keep the ball moving. You can't expect the other party to do this. Whatever you're working on is probably not as important to them as it is to you. The key is continuous connection.

Think of it this way: If you're out fishing and have a fish hooked, you need to maintain constant tension on the line. If you let out too much slack, the fish will spit out the hook and swim away. The same is true with people. You need to maintain momentum to realize your goals.

As an individual consultant, my plate can fill with work. I still take calls with prospective clients about new potential business, but I sometimes don't have time to pursue these opportunities. I may not put much energy into the follow-up. Not surprisingly, those opportunities almost never come to fruition. That's because I did not maintain momentum.

If I do want the business, I will constantly connect with the prospect to offer information and insights of value. This results in exponentially higher levels of success.

What are you working on now that depends on someone else to accomplish your goal? What can you do to create and maintain momentum?

RULE

19

Stay Organized

Back in the day, a company had one person to answer the phone, another to create the graphics, and yet another person to handle travel plans. Now we do all of it ourselves, including trying to stay on top of texts, IMs, email, and phone calls. Sometimes it feels like there's no time to even do the work.

The first thing you need to do is prioritize what's most important. Stephen Covey, author of *The Seven Habits of Highly Effective People*, says, "Put first things first." At work, I believe that means staying focused on the tasks that propel the company's top objectives or your personal brand.

To manage priorities and time, I have found it necessary to have a day-to-day organizing system. I've had different systems over the years, and while you don't need my system, you need a system.

My system is influenced by David Allen, the author of *Getting Things Done*. His premise is to get things out of your head and into the system. If you have a system, you don't have to worry about things falling through the cracks. This removes a lot of anxiety.

The system includes:

- **A Notebook:** It can be physical or digital. I use Evernote.

- **Project List:** This is not a task list. It's a list of all your projects – anything that takes more than a few steps to complete.

- **To-Do List:** This is the task list. I break down each project into steps, and those steps turn into tasks.

- **Calendar:** This is the main thing I look at every day. I will often move tasks into my calendar, so I can complete them during a specified time.

- **Email Folders:** Besides my inbox and separate project folders, I have an Actions folder (emails I know are important but can't handle right now) and a Commitments folder (stuff people owe me).

Every Friday, I have a meeting with myself. First, I go through my notebook and review all my notes from the past week. If there are action items, I add them to my task list.

Then I review my project list and ask myself, "What needs to be done next for this project?" I add those to my task list.

Next, I review the tasks on my to-do list and see if I checked everything off.

Then I review my calendar from the past week, which can serve as a reminder to create tasks. For example, the calendar is a trigger for me to assign a follow-up task from a customer meeting.

After that, I look at the upcoming week in my calendar. I may schedule tasks in preparation for a meeting (reviewing background information, for example). I also block time off on my calendar to get actual work done.

Each day you should be tackling activities that address your weekly priorities, which ultimately enables you to achieve your quarterly and yearly goals.

(When I work, I turn off all notifications, buzzes, and beeps. It's difficult to be creative with constant interruptions.)

Finally, I go through my Actions email folder and respond to all outstanding messages. Then I check my Commitments e-mail folder — did I get everything I needed? And if I haven't heard from the recipient in a few days, I'll check in with them.

Now, let's talk more about "priorities." For the most part, the time you spend each day should be guided by your top priorities. To do this, you need a priorities list.

I recommend having a list of your top priorities for the year – this might only be one or two broad goals. Then every three months, create a priorities list for the upcoming quarter.

You should not have more than three to five priorities at any given time. Your quarterly priorities should represent milestone achievements like getting a key piece of a larger project completed, launching a new service, or securing a key relationship.

During your weekly organizational meetings, write down your top priorities for the week. Do the items on your to-do list and calendar support your quarterly priorities? They should.

Each day you should be tackling activities that address your weekly priorities, which ultimately enables you to achieve your quarterly and yearly goals.

RULE

20

Keep Learning

When I was younger, I was sure I knew it all. I remember taking a class on business management when I was in college, and on the first day I thought, "Management? Don't you just tell people what to do?" I quickly learned how complex the topic is. As I've gotten older, I'm continually reminded how much I don't know.

College is just a starting point for your career. Think about all the schooling doctors go through — undergrad, medical school, residency — just to start practicing medicine. Throughout their careers, they must keep up with licensing requirements, technology changes, and new or better procedures.

Every industry is changing all the time. When I started out in marketing, I mailed five-inch floppy disks and physical newsletters. (I'm really going to age myself here: If we needed to transfer data from one person to another, we did "floppy disk swaps" — we pulled one disk out of one computer and put it into another — because there were no computer networks.)

No matter how much technology changes around you, the 21 rules in this book will always be applicable. They are universal principals for you to maximize your effectiveness, regardless of your job or work environment. But even still, they need to be revisited and constantly studied. Though I wrote them, I am always learning more and improving my understanding of them.

What can you do to keep learning? What can you do to be better?

Read books, articles, and blog posts. Talk to people — people with years (or decades) of experience. Listen to podcasts. And don't forget to share your own ideas to support someone else's learning.

RULE

21

Luck Is a Skill

Luck doesn't happen by chance. People get lucky because they put themselves out there, look for the right opportunities and know when to strike.

Think about it this way: You can only win at poker if you play a hand. As Kenny Rogers sings in "The Gambler," you have to know when to hold 'em and know when to fold 'em. There are odds in any card game based on where you are at the table and the cards you are dealt. Play enough, and at the right moment you will win.

Once I went on a big birding trip with my dad to the Dry Tortugas off Key West, Florida — a mecca for bird watchers. On one island, we saw a huge gathering of people. We walked up and quietly asked, "What's going on?"

"It's a yellow-faced grassquit!"

I am not a birder, so I didn't know what a big deal it was until someone explained that this was the third time EVER the bird was spotted in the continental United States.

Was this sighting lucky? By my definition, yes. Go where the birds are often enough, and eventually you will spot a rare bird.

At work, put yourself into a position that will lead to success. The people who actively network get the new job. The people who take on high-profile projects that demonstrate their capabilities get the promotion. The people who make a positive impact get the raise. These people also have suffered failures, but you don't see that. You see only luck.

In Chapter Four, I told you how I landed a job at Citrix — persistence, via nonstop outreach to the CEO Roger Roberts. As you may recall, one day I called his office and he picked up the phone. Was it luck? I had been calling him every other day for two months. Eventually he was going to answer the phone.

Not every opportunity that comes your way will be the right opportunity. It's OK to say no. If you are dealt a bad hand, fold. If you are offered a job that isn't right for you, don't take it. The right opportunity hasn't presented itself yet.

Over time, as you grow in your expertise, confidence and experience, you begin to understand which opportunities are the right ones. Keep your eye out for them, because the right ones may have an immense impact on the trajectory of your life.

Now, go out into the world and make it happen.

Takeaways

The 21 Rules

Review these rules on a regular basis, until they become a natural part of your working style:

1. **Build your personal brand:** Decide what you want to be known for, and then intentionally build and maintain your brand.

2. **Give people what they need:** Tap into your expertise to give people the solution they need, not necessarily what they want.

3. **Expectations and communications:** When you commit to something, deliver on it. And once you commit, communicate progress.

4. **Be proactive:** Look for opportunities to bring additional value to the organization and make things happen.

5. **Persistence pays:** If you want a certain job or project, don't give up. Use your persuasive powers to get the other party to say yes.

6. **Attack from the top:** When necessary, go straight to people in positions of authority. They have the credibility and power to get things done.

7. **Prepare for every meeting:** Meetings are opportunities to move the ball forward on a project or decision. Never step into one without first organizing your thoughts and reviewing your notes.

8. **Always take notes:** Taking notes during a meeting is the best way to recall, retain and even learn new information.

9. **Set high standards:** If you're going to exert the energy to do something, do it right.

10. **Go slow to go fast:** Spend time learning the fundamentals, collecting the information, asking questions and building trust.

11. **Write it to understand it:** Writing down your thoughts and ideas allows you to process them, better understand them and gain clarity.

12. **Write well:** Learn how to effectively organize and succinctly communicate your ideas.

13. **Everyone's a salesperson:** No matter your job title, you will be selling — an idea, a product, yourself. To do this effectively, you must listen, confirm your target's needs, align your pitch to their needs, and share evidence that supports your claims.

14. **How to build a team:** When building a team, focus on skill set, attitude, and team fit over the resume.

15. **Treat everyone with dignity:** Remember that we are all human. No matter the situation, treat others with compassion and respect.

16. **Respond, don't react:** When you're challenged, take a deep breath, pause and ask a question.

17. **Questions are your secret weapons:** Questions can soften a statement, create a dialogue, and allow you to make a point without sounding accusatory.

18. **Maintain your momentum:** Once you get forward movement on a job, project, or opportunity, keep the ball moving by staying in constant communication.

19. **Stay organized:** Put a system in place to manage priorities and your time to ensure nothing falls through the cracks.

20. **Keep learning:** Every industry is constantly changing. Commit to learning more and doing better.

21. **Luck is a skill:** If you constantly pursue opportunities and are willing to accept failure, "luck" will certainly come your way.

Recommended Reading:

These are some of the classics which have taught and influenced me:

- *The 7 Habits of Highly Effective People* (Stephen Covey)

- *Benjamin Franklin: An American Life* (Walter Isaacson)

- *Getting Things Done* (David Allen)

- *Getting to Yes* (Roger Fisher and William Ury)

- *How to Win Friends and Influence People* (Dale Carnegie)

- *Negotiate This* (Herb Cohen)

- *Radical Acceptance* (Tara Brach)

Acknowledgements

I never would have been able to write this book without many excellent mentors over the years. Special thanks to my father, Barry Heimlich, who taught me the importance of perseverance from a very early age. And thank you to my mother, Carole Busch, who is the best listener I know. She instilled in me the importance of treating people with dignity.

Thank you to my grandfather, Papa Charlie. His memory still inspires me daily.

I was also blessed with some excellent bosses over the years, who I learned from directly and just by watching them — especially Denis Russ, Roland Garcia, Mark Templeton, Roger Roberts, and Nicola Sanna.

Thank you also to Monika Jansen for her remarkable talent and guidance throughout the writing process. Also thank you to my reviewers — Cindy Goodman, Liran Gordon, Shiri Huber and Zach Jacobs — for their invaluable feedback.

Finally, special thanks to my wife Cheryl, who not only helped edit this book, but is the amazing "Organizer" on my team.

About the Author:

Daniel Heimlich is a businessman, marketer, and mentor. During a 35-year career, he worked his way up from selling printing services to the head of marketing for a $400M division of a global technology and services company. He has been employed as an individual contributor, and has managed large teams. Today he runs a marketing consulting practice, advising entrepreneurs and CEOs at early-stage technology companies throughout the United States. He regularly volunteers as a coach for young professionals, helping them navigate their careers and job hunts. In addition, he is a board advisor and mentor for the Network for Teaching Entrepreneurship (NFTE), which supports economically disadvantaged teens in the Washington, D.C. region. Daniel lives with his family in Potomac, Maryland.

To contact Daniel, send him an email at:
Success@DanielHeimlich.com